孔子学院总部 /
国家汉办汉语国际推广成都基地规划教材

走进天府系列教材【成都印象】

吃川菜

Let's Eat Sichuan Food

西 南 财 经 大 学
汉语国际推广成都基地 著

西南财经大学出版社
中国·成都

西 南 财 经 大 学
汉语国际推广成都基地 著

总策划 涂文涛

策 划
李永强

主 编
梁 婷 白巧燕

编 者
《成都印象·游成都》 胡倩琳
《成都印象·居成都》 郑 莹
《成都印象·吃川菜》 谢 娟 王 新
《成都印象·品川茶》 肖 静
《成都印象·饮川酒》 谢 娟
《成都印象·看川剧》 郑 莹
《成都印象·绣蜀绣》 谢 娟
《成都印象·梦王国之蜀国》 蒋林益 胡佩迦
《成都印象·悟道教》 沙 莎 吕 彦 陈 茉
《成都印象·练武术》 邓 帆 刘 亚

审 订 冯卫东

英文翻译
Alexander Demmelhuber

Introduction

The Sichuan cuisine is one of the eight major Chinese cuisines. What we call "Sichuan cuisine" is divided into three styles: Shanghe style, represented by Chengdu, Meishan and other regions; Xiaohe style, represented by Zigong, Neijiang and other regions; and Xiahe style, represented by Chongqing, Wanzhou and other regions. Although these styles are all Sichuanese cooking, they have developed by themselves through the centuries and ultimately produced special and distinct flavors. As the Sichuanese like to say, "Each dish has its own style; a hundred dishes have a hundred different flavors." In 2011, Chengdu was awarded the title of "UNESCO City of Gastronomy" (only six cities worldwide were considered), which is the world's affirmation of Sichuan cuisine and its culture.

Let's Eat Sichuan Food is one part of the "Impressions of Chengdu" textbook series, which is promoted by the Chengdu Base of Confucius Institute Headquarters and published by the Southwestern University of Finance and Economics. This book contains 6 units, which are designed on the basis of the Confucius Institute Headquarters'/Hanban's "International Curriculum for Chinese Language Education" (hereinafter referred to as "Curriculum"), as can be seen, for example, on vocabulary and language points used, and ensures that this textbook is held to scientific, systematic and rigorous standards.

This book begins with the history and preparation methods of Sichuan cuisine, introduces some signature dishes as well as some nostalgic snacks the Sichuanese grew up with. Of course, we will also take a look at the "soul" of Sichuan cuisine: chili bean paste. Last will be an overview of the Sichuan Museum.

This book's vocabulary follows the "Outline Vocabulary of the New HSK" and the lessons contained herein are designed for readers at the HSK 4 level or above. For ease of understanding, the units are presented in narrative and dialog forms.

Hopefully, you will enjoy *Let's Eat Sichuan Food* and we are looking forward to any criticism or suggestions you might have. Hanban gave us much help and support during editing of this book and we would like to take this opportunity to express our gratitude.

前言

　　"川菜"是中国八大菜系之一。我们现在所说的川菜分为三个流派：以成都、眉山等地区为代表的上河帮川菜；以自贡、内江等地区为代表的小河帮川菜；以重庆、万州等地区为代表的下河帮川菜。虽然都是川菜，但是各个流派又各有千秋，最终形成了川菜"一菜一格""百菜百味"的特殊风味。2010 年，四川省会成都市被联合国教科文组织授予"世界美食之都"的荣誉称号(全球仅 6 个城市入选)，这是世界对川菜以及川菜文化的肯定。

　　《吃川菜》是西南财经大学汉语国际推广成都基地推出的《成都印象》系列教材之一。全书共 6 课，以孔子学院总部／国家汉办的《国际汉语教学通用课程大纲》为基本编写依据，涉及大纲中的大量词汇、语言点等指标，以保证教材的科学性、系统性和严谨性。

　　本书从川菜的历史和做法入手，介绍了川菜的一些代表菜，以及一些深藏在记忆深处的川味小吃，当然还有川菜的"灵魂"——豆瓣酱的介绍，最后简略介绍了川菜博物馆的情况。本书所使用词汇参照《新汉语水平考试词汇大纲》编排设计，适宜具有 HSK4 级以上水平的读者阅读。为了便于理解，全书以叙述和对话两种表现形式呈现。

　　希望您能喜欢我们的《吃川菜》这本教材，也希望您对本书提出批评和建议。本书的编写得到了国家汉办的大力支持和帮助，在此一并表示感谢。

目录

第一课
Lesson 1

【辣妹子不怕辣】
【The Spicy Girls can Handle the Spice】

① 歌 词　gēcí
② 四 川　Sìchuān
③ 重 庆　Chóngqìng
④ 湖 南　Húnán
⑤ 贵 州　Guìzhōu
⑥ 比 如　bǐrú
⑦ 潮 湿　cháoshī
⑧ 汗　　hàn
⑨ 湿 气　shīqì
⑩ 寒 气　hánqì
⑪ 排　　pái

江一华：
　　小西，你在听什么歌？

文小西：
　　我在听《辣妹子》，很好听，歌词也很有意思。

江一华：
　　"辣妹子"？是什么意思？

大 萌：
　　"妹子"就是"女孩子"。四川、重庆、湖南、贵州的人非常喜欢吃辣的东西，我们把这四个地方的女孩叫"辣妹子"。

江一华：
　　为什么这几个地方的人特别喜欢吃辣的呢？

大 萌：
　　他们喜欢吃辣跟环境和天气有关系。比如在四川，常常下雨，空气非常潮湿，人们生活在这样的环境里，容易生病。所以在饭菜里加点儿辣椒，吃的时候就会全身出汗，那些湿气和寒气会跟着汗一起排出去。

① 锅　　　　guō
② 麻　　　　má
③ 咸　　　　xián
④ 汤 汁　　 tāngzhī
⑤ 九宫格　 jiǔgōnggé
⑥ 传 统　　chuántǒng
⑦ 牛 油　　niúyóu
⑧ 红汤锅　 hóngtāng guō
⑨ 清汤锅　 qīngtāng guō
⑩ 鸳鸯锅　 yuānyāng guō
⑪ 长 江　　Chángjiāng
⑫ 水 牛　　shuǐniú
⑬ 味 道　　wèidào
⑭ 煮　　　　zhǔ

【一】火锅

　　重庆火锅的锅很特别——一个大锅，锅里是又麻又辣又咸的汤汁，叫锅底，再放上九宫格，一格里放一种菜。大家坐在一起热热闹闹地吃。

　　传统的重庆火锅里面有很多牛油。现在的重庆火锅里牛油少了很多，锅底也有很多种——红汤锅、清汤锅、鸳鸯锅等。红汤锅是辣的锅底，有微辣、中辣、特辣等。清汤锅是不辣的锅底，鸳鸯锅是一半辣一半不辣的锅底。

　　最早的火锅是重庆长江边的工人们吃的。那时，他们所食水牛肉虽然便宜，但是味道不太好，需要用麻辣的火锅来煮。现在火锅的菜有很多，几乎所有能吃的东西都可以放在火锅里。

火锅该怎么吃？把所有东西一起放进去煮？如果你是这样想的，你就错了。火锅的吃法有两种：一是煮，把鱼、肉丸等需要很长时间才能熟的菜放进去煮；二是烫，把毛肚、鸭肠等很快就能熟的菜烫一烫就可以吃了，而且不同的菜烫的时间也不同。一般来说，吃火锅的时候是先吃肉后吃蔬菜。

火锅到了不同的地方，就有了不同的风格，比如重庆火锅和成都火锅。首先，油不一样。重庆火锅里有很多牛油，一份锅底里 60% ～ 80% 都是牛油。成都火锅使用菜籽油，而且锅底里的油很少。所以很多重庆人把成都火锅叫作"清油火锅"。其次，蘸料[①]不一样。重庆火锅的蘸料一般就是芝麻油加蒜泥，而成都火锅的蘸料非常多——芝麻油、蒜泥、耗油、豆豉，还有各种酱。最后，菜不一样。重庆火锅主要吃肉，成都火锅里蔬菜的种类也很多。

作为一种美食，火锅已经成了四川的名片，所以有人说"到了四川如果不吃火锅，就等于没有到过四川"。

⑮ 烫　　tàng
⑯ 风　格　fēnggé
⑰ 毛　肚　máodǔ
⑱ 菜籽油　càizǐ yóu
⑲ 蘸　料　zhànliào
⑳ 芝麻油　zhīma yóu
㉑ 蒜　泥　suànní
㉒ 耗　油　háoyóu
㉓ 豆　豉　dòuchǐ
㉔ 酱　　Jiàng

① 蘸料：吃火锅或者串串的时候使用的调料碟。将菜品煮熟后放在蘸料里，一方面是通过蘸料里的芝麻油将菜迅速降温，另一方面是通过蘸料里的调料让菜味道更好。

【二】串串

①起源于	qǐyuán yú
②代 表	dàibiǎo
③之 一	zhīyī
④竹 签	zhúqiān
⑤串	chuàn
⑥买 单	mǎidān
⑦油 碟	yóudié
⑧干 碟	gāndié
⑨辣 椒	làjiāo
⑩花椒面	huājiāo miàn
⑪调 料	tiáoliào
⑫火	huǒ
⑬高 档	gāodàng

串串，也叫"小火锅"，起源于四川眉山，是四川味道的代表之一。串串的味道与火锅差不多——麻、辣、鲜、香。不过串串最大的特点是它所有的菜都用竹签串成串，你想吃什么就拿什么。买单的时候老板按照竹签的数量或重量收钱。串串的另外一个特点就是它的蘸料分油碟和干碟。油碟以芝麻油和蒜泥为主，适合不太能吃辣的人。干碟以辣椒面、花椒面等调料为主，适合喜欢吃辣的人。

串串大概有30年的历史，美味又便宜，非常受欢迎，也因此很快地火了起来。在成都，不管是街边小巷，还是高档商场，都可以看到串串店。

【三】冒菜

①群	qún
②狂 欢	kuánghuān
③冒 菜	màocài
④熟	shú
⑤舀	yǎo
⑥勺	sháo
⑦撒	sǎ
⑧葱 花	cōnghuā
⑨香 菜	xiāngcài
⑩俱 全	jùquán
⑪热腾腾	rèténgténg
⑫上 火	shànghuǒ
⑬伤 胃	shāngwèi

有人说，火锅是一群人的狂欢，而冒菜是一个人的火锅。冒菜是什么？许多第一次来成都的人都不知道。冒菜不是一种菜，而是一种做菜的方法——先把菜放在锅里烫熟，然后倒进碗里，最后舀一勺汤汁，这就是"冒"。冒菜的碗里需要先放好调料，然后放入菜和汤汁，最后撒上葱花、香菜等，一份色香味俱全的热腾腾的冒菜就做好了。

冒菜和火锅、串串最大的不同就是它的汤汁。冒菜的汤汁是用十几种中草药加上各种调料做的，不上火，不伤胃，还可以直接喝。而火锅、串串的锅底应该没有人敢喝吧。

Jiang Yihua: Xiaoxi, what song are you listening to?

Wen Xiaoxi: I'm listening to "Spicy Girls". I like it quite a lot. The lyrics are also interesting!

Jiang Yihua: "Spicy Girls"? What does that mean?

Da Meng: In Sichuan, Chongqing, Hunan and Guizhou, people love hot and spicy tastes. We call the girls and women from these four places "spicy girls".

Jiang Yihua: Why do the people from these places love eating spicy food so much?

Da Meng: This has something to do with the environment and climate. For example, it rains often in Sichuan, so the climate is very damp. In this kind of environment, it is easy to get sick. This is why they add chilis to their food, making them sweat during eating. The moisture and cold are secreted out together with the sweat.

Part 1 【 Hot Pot 】

The pot of Chongqing's hot pot is very special: a cauldron, inside a ma spicy and salty soup called the base; on top of that, the nine-square grid: one dish in every grid. Everybody has a good time eating.

In traditional hot pot is a lot of butter. Nowadays there is a lot less butter in Chongqing hot pot and a wide range of soup bases: red soup pot, clear soup pot, mandarin duck pot and so on. Red soup pot uses a spicy soup base with varying pungencies: mild, medium, extra, etc. Clear soup pot is not a spicy soup base. The mandarin duck pot uses two soup bases: One is spicy; the other one is not.

The earliest hot pot was eaten by workers at the Yangtze River in Chongqing. Since they had no money, they could only eat water buffalo. Although water buffalo meat is cheap, it does not taste great, which made it necessary to be cooked in a tingling and spicy hot pot. Now there are many hot pot dishes. For almost everything edible, you can put it in a hot pot.

How do you eat hot pot? Put everything together to cook? If that is what you are thinking, you are wrong. There are two ways to eat hot pot. One is boiling: you put in fish, meatballs and other dishes that take a long time to get done and let them boil; the other one is blanching: you put tripes, duck gizzards and other dishes that take a short time to get done and let them blanch for a little while, then they are ready to be eaten. Furthermore, different dishes also take differing amounts of time to blanch. For hot pot eating in general, you first have meat and vegetables afterwards.

Every place has a different style of hot pot; just take Chongqing Hot Pot and Chengdu Hot Pot as examples. First, the fat used is different. There is a lot of butter in Chongqing Hot Pot: one soup base serving consists of 60% to 80% butter. Chengdu Hot Pot uses rapeseed oil and very little oil in its soup base. This is why a lot of Chongqing people call Chengdu Hot Pot "Vegetable Oil Hot Pot". Second, the dips differ. The dips for Chongqing Hot Pot generally consist of sesame oil, mashed garlic, oyster sauce, fermented black soybeans and various soy sauces. Last, the dishes are different. Chongqing Hot Pot is mainly about meat, while there are also many kinds of vegetables to be eaten in Chengdu Hot Pot.

As a delicacy, hot pot has become Sichuan's signature food, which is why some people say, "If you go to Sichuan and don't have some hot pot, that's as if you've never actually been there."

① dip: condiments in a saucer for eating hot pot and chuanchuan. Place cooked dishes into the dip while make them quickly cool through the sesame oil inside the dip on the one hand, while the condiments inside the dip make the dishes taste even better.

Part 2 【Chuanchuan】

Chuanchuan, also called "small hot pot", stems from Meishan, Sichuan, and is one of Sichuan cuisine's signature foods. Their flavor is almost as the same as hot pot's: ma, spicy, umami and fragrant. What makes them so special is that all their dishes are stringed together on bamboo skewers. You can pick and choose and eat whatever you want. When you pay the bill, the owner collects the money according to the number of bamboo skewers. Chuanchuan are also special in their dips, which are divided into oil dips and dry dips. Oil dips are based on sesame oil and mashed garlic and are suitable for those who cannot eat spicy food. Dry dips are based on condiments such as chili pepper and Sichuan pepper powders and are suitable for those who like spicy food.

Chuanchuan goes back about 30 years. They are delicious and cheap, have been incredibly well-received and thus spread fast. In Chengdu, be it in the streets or in upscale shopping malls, you can see chuanchuan shops everywhere.

Part 3 【Maocai】

Some say that hot pot is a group's revelry and maocai is one person's hot pot. What is maocai? Many who come to Chengdu for their first time do not know. Maocai is not some dish. It is a preparation method: First, put the dish into a pot and let it blanch until done, then pour it into a bowl. Last, pour a ladle of soup on top: This is called "mao" (cover). The condiments have to be put into the bowl first before the dish and soup are added. Chopped green onions, coriander and so on are finally sprinkled on top – and then there it is: a steaming hot bowl of maocai that smells, looks and tastes great!

The biggest difference between maocai, hot pot and chuanchuan are their soups. Maocai soup uses dozens of Chinese medical herbs added with a variety of seasonings, which does not build up excessive internal heat in the human body and does not hurt the stomach. You may even drink it. Hot pot's and chuanchuan's soup bases only few would dare to drink.

词语

锅 guō pot	串 chuàn string together	热腾腾 rèténgténg steaming hot; piping hot

gē cí 歌 词	lyrics	bǐ rú 比 如	for example
cháo shī 潮 湿	damp	hàn 汗	sweat
shī qì 湿 气	moisture	hán qì 寒 气	cold
pái 排	discharge; discrete; eject	má 麻	(sensation caused by Sichuan pepper) ma；numbing; tingling
xián 咸	salty	tāng zhī 汤 汁	soup; broth

chuán tǒng 传 统	traditional
zhǔ 煮	boil; cook
fēng gé 风 格	style
dài biǎo 代 表	represent
mǎi dān 买 单	pay the bill
huǒ 火	hot (popular)
qún 群	crowd; group
shú 熟	cooked; done

wèi dào 味 道	flavor
tàng 烫	blanch
qǐ yuán yú 起 源 于	stem from; originate from
zhī yī 之 一	one of (sth.)
tiáo liào 调 料	condiment; seasoning; flavoring
gāo dàng 高 档	upscale; high grade
kuáng huān 狂 欢	revelry; carnival
yǎo 舀	ladle out

sháo 勺	spoon; ladle
jù quán 俱 全	complete; entire

să 撒	sprinkle
shàng huǒ 上 火	(TCM) suffer from excessive internal heat (with such symptoms as constipation, conjunctivitis, and inflammation of the nasal and oral cavities)

专 有 名 词

1. 四川　/Sìchuān / Sichuan

2. 重庆　/Chóngqìng / Chongqing

3. 湖南　/ Húnán / Hunan

4. 贵州　/Guìzhōu / Guizhou

5. 九宫格　/ jiǔgōnggé / nine square grid

6. 长江　/ Chángjiāng / Yangtze River

语言点

1. 首先……其次……最后……
2. 以……为主……
3. 不管……，还是……，都…

思考

1. 你能吃辣吗？你喜欢吃辣吗？

2. 你家乡菜辣不辣？川菜的辣和你家乡菜的辣有什么不一样？

3. 你吃过四川火锅吗？你吃的是重庆火锅还是成都火锅？为什么？

4. 你们国家有火锅吗？跟四川火锅有什么区别？

5. 串串也叫"小火锅"，那么串串和火锅有什么区别呢？

6. 火锅、串串、冒菜，除了汤汁不一样以外，还有什么不一样？请说明。

第二课

Lesson 2 【川菜百味】

【Sichuan Cuisine: A Lot of Different Flavors】

① 称　　　　chēng
② 百菜百味　bǎicàibǎiwèi
③ 麻辣　　　málà
④ 酸辣　　　suānlà
⑤ 甜辣　　　tiánlà
⑥ 鱼香　　　yúxiāng
⑦ 怪味　　　guàiwèi
⑧ 大多数　　dàduōshù

文小西：
我们一说到川菜就会想到麻辣。川菜里都是麻辣的味道吗？

江一华：
应该也有不辣的，但是可能不多吧。

大　萌：
川菜被称为"百菜百味"，有很多种味道呢。除了麻辣以外，还有酸辣、甜辣、鱼香、怪味等。

江一华：
做川菜麻烦吗？

大　萌：
不麻烦。大多数川菜都很简单，很容易学会。

【一】最经典的麻辣味

文小西：
一华，昨天我吃了一个又麻又辣、好吃又好看的菜。

江一华：
真的吗？什么菜这么特别？

文小西：

辣子鸡。那个菜是用红的干辣椒、花椒和鸡肉一起炒的。红红的辣椒看起来特别漂亮。

江一华：

我以前不喜欢吃辣，但是现在很喜欢。我觉得四川人真的很厉害，能把麻和辣搭配成这么好吃的味道。

大萌：

麻辣是川菜里最特别的味道，一些外地人来了四川以后不喜欢麻辣，不过也有很多外地人爱上了麻辣，把麻辣带回了自己的家乡。

文小西：

是啊。我就很喜欢麻辣，我给家人寄了麻辣调料，妈妈说很好吃。

江一华：

大萌，川菜里还有一些什么麻辣的菜呢？给我们介绍一下吧。

大萌：

川菜中麻辣味道的菜很多，比如回锅肉、麻婆豆腐、水煮鱼等。

文小西：

水煮鱼？名字听起来一点儿也不辣啊。

① 厉害　　lìhai
② 搭配　　dāpèi
③ 外地人　wàidì rén
④ 家乡　　jiāxiāng
⑤ 回锅肉　huíguōròu
⑥ 麻婆豆腐 mápó dòufu
⑦ 水煮鱼　shuǐzhǔyú
⑧ 重　　　zhòng

大 萌：

> 虽然叫水煮，但是麻辣味儿非常重，吃的时候有可能把你辣哭。现在的川菜里，水煮的菜有很多，比如水煮牛肉、水煮肉片等。

回锅肉

回锅肉可以说是"川菜之王"，它属于川菜里的家常菜，不是特别麻辣，在四川几乎家家都会做，人人都爱吃。简单地说，回锅肉就是把煮好的肉再放回锅里炒一次。为什么要这么麻烦地回锅呢？以前四川人每个月都要用煮熟的五花肉祭祀，祭祀完以后，又舍不得浪费这些被神和祖先"吃"过的肉，于是四川人就把这些肉切成片回锅炒一下，做成了"回锅肉"。就是这么简单的做法，却做出了"川菜之王"，这是所有川菜馆必备的一道菜，也是所有四川人都喜欢的一道菜。

① 属 于　shǔyú
② 祭 祀　jìsì
③ 舍不得　shě·bu·de
④ 浪 费　làngfèi
⑤ 祖 先　zǔxiān
⑥ 片　piàn
⑦ 道　dào

麻：★★★
辣：★★★

麻婆豆腐

　　麻婆豆腐是川菜的代表菜之一，已经有一百五十几年的历史了。那时候在成都万福桥边有一家小饭店，老板娘姓陈，因为脸上有很多麻子，所以大家叫她"陈麻婆"。陈麻婆最拿手的一道菜就是做豆腐，她把豆腐和肉末、辣椒、花椒、豆瓣酱等一起烧，烧出来的豆腐非常好吃，大家都很喜欢。因为这道菜又麻又辣，老板娘又叫陈麻婆，所以大家叫这个菜"麻婆豆腐"。

①万福桥　　Wàn Fú Qiáo
②老板娘　　láobǎnniáng
③麻　子　　mázi
④拿　手　　náshǒu
⑤豆　腐　　dòufu
⑥末　　　　mò
⑦豆瓣酱　　dòubànjiàng
⑧烧　　　　shāo

麻：★★★★★
辣：★★★★

【二】辣和其他味道的组合

江一华：
　　四川人真的不怕辣。

文小西：
　　如果怕辣，就不是辣妹子了吧。

大　萌：
　　辣妹子爱吃辣，所以辣妹子把川菜的"辣"做出了很多不同的味道。

文小西：
　　不同的辣？什么意思？

①组　合　　zǔhé
②醋　　　　cù
③经　典　　jīngdiǎn
④酸　菜　　suāncài
⑤泡　椒　　pàojiāo
⑥酸　　　　suān
⑦宫保鸡丁　gōngbǎo jīdīng

大 萌：

很多外地人以为川菜只有麻辣，其实川菜的"辣"是有很多变化的——酸辣、甜辣、鱼香等。

江—华：

酸辣？是用醋和辣椒做的吗？

大 萌：

有些地方的菜里的酸辣是用醋，不过川菜里经典的酸辣菜是"酸菜鱼"。这道菜是用酸菜和泡椒做的，又酸又辣。

文小西：

甜辣我知道，宫保鸡丁就是甜辣味儿的。可是"鱼香"是什么？

大 萌：

"鱼香"是川菜一种独特的味道。"鱼香肉丝"就是一道名菜。

宫保鸡丁

以前四川有个官员，叫丁宝桢。丁宝桢是一个"吃货"，他不仅喜欢去吃各地的特色菜，而且还常常自己发明一些菜的做法。丁宝桢非常喜欢吃鸡肉和花生米，又特别喜欢吃辣味儿。他把鸡肉、红辣椒和花生米一起炒，味道非常好。后来丁宝桢当了宫保，大家都叫他丁宫保，把他发明的这道菜叫"宫保鸡丁"。丁宝桢去世后，这道菜被四川官员献给皇上，成为御用名菜之一。

现在的宫保鸡丁成了川菜里的家常菜之一，这道菜甜中有辣，辣中有甜，受到了大家的欢迎。

① 官 员　　guānyuán
② 丁宝桢　　Dīng Bǎozhēn
③ 吃 货　　chīhuò
④ 各 地　　gèdì
⑤ 发 明　　fāmíng
⑥ 花生米　　huāshēng mǐ
⑦ 宫 保　　gōngbǎo
⑧ 去 世　　qùshì
⑨ 献　　　xiàn
⑩ 御　　　yù

甜：★　　　辣：★★

鱼香肉丝

大多数人第一次吃这道菜时都会有一个疑问——鱼香肉丝里为什么没有鱼？如果你也有这个疑问，那么只能说明你被这道菜的名字骗了。"鱼香"是川菜特有的一种味道。

"鱼香"的菜里看不到鱼，它的味道也跟鱼没有关系，只是用了一些做鱼的方法。以前有个人做鱼的时候，准备的调料太多了，又舍不得浪费，所以用来炒肉丝，没想到味道非常好。后来越来越多的人这样炒肉丝，并给了这道菜新的名字——鱼香肉丝。

"鱼香肉丝"是用肉丝和泡椒、大葱、糖、醋等调料一起炒的菜，所以，"鱼香"味儿到底是什么样的味道呢？

① 鱼香肉丝　Yú Xiāng Ròu Sī
② 疑问　yíwèn
③ 炒　chǎo
④ 大葱　dàcōng
⑤ 到底　dàodǐ

甜：★★　　酸：★★　　辣：★

【三】四川怪味

川菜里有一道菜叫"怪味鸡"，对很多人来说，吃怪味鸡以前，非常好奇什么样的味道能叫"怪味"。吃了怪味鸡以后，却又说不出这个"怪味"到底是什么味道。

如果说到"味道"，大多数人会想到麻、辣、咸、甜、酸等，可是作为吃货的四川人，怎么可能满足于这么简单的味道呢？聪明的四川人找到了麻、辣、咸、甜、酸的平衡点，把五种味道放在一起，听起

① 怪　guài
② 好奇　hàoqí
③ 作为　zuòwéi
④ 满足于　mǎnzú yú
⑤ 平衡点　pínghéng diǎn
⑥ 却　què
⑦ 意外　yìwài
⑧ 大概　dàgài
⑨ 胡豆　hú dòu

来很奇怪，吃起来却是一种意外的美味，他们把这种味道叫作"怪味"。

怪味大概出现在七十几年前，最早是因为重庆的"怪味胡豆"而出名，后来慢慢成为川菜的一种特别的味道。《四川怪味菜》这本书里介绍了 200 个怪味菜品，每道菜的做法都不太一样，但是每个菜都很"怪"。

怪：★★★★★

【四】没有辣椒的川菜

> **文小西：**
> 只有吃过川菜才知道，辣椒也能这么好吃。

> **江一华：**
> 而且辣味可以和那么多别的味道完美结合，真是美味。

> **文小西：**
> 来四川以前，我觉得每天吃辣的菜，我会活不下去。现在我觉得，离开了辣我才会活不下去。

> **江一华：**
> 你离不开辣椒，你真的变成四川人了。

① 完 美　　wánměi
② 结 合　　jiéhé
③ 活　　　　huó
④ 糖醋排骨　tángcù páigǔ
⑤ 男女老少　nánnǚ lǎoshào
⑥ 眉 山　　Méishān
⑦ 美 容　　měiróng
⑧ 东坡肘子　Dōngpō Zhǒuzi
⑨ 梅干菜　　Méigān Cài
⑩ 烧 白　　shāobái

大萌:

跟很多外地人一样，你们都觉得四川人一定离不开辣吧，其实不是这样的。大多数四川人喜欢吃辣，也能把辣味的菜做得特别好吃，但不是只会做辣味的菜，也不是离不开辣。

文小西:

真的吗？川菜里也有不辣的菜吗？

大萌:

当然。比如糖醋排骨，酸酸甜甜，男女老少都爱吃；比如眉山的美容菜"东坡肘子"；比如用五花肉和梅干菜做的"烧白"。

东坡肘子

苏东坡，北宋大文学家，也是美食家。不过东坡肘子的发明者却不是苏东坡自己，而是他的妻子王弗。王弗是四川眉山人，有一次王弗在炖肘子的时候，一不小心，就炖干了水，肘子也有点儿焦了。为了掩盖肘子的焦味儿，王弗加了很多调料，小心地又煮了一次。没想到这个焦黄的肘子得到了美食家苏东坡的赞美，后来越来越多的人知道了"东坡肘子"的做法，"东坡肘子"成了川菜里的名菜之一。

① 苏东坡　Sū Dōngpō
② 北　宋　Běi Sòng
③ 文学家　wénxuéjiā
④ 美食家　měishíjiā
⑤ 王　弗　Wáng Fú
⑥ 炖　　　dùn
⑦ 干　　　gān
⑧ 焦　　　jiāo
⑨ 掩　盖　yǎngài
⑩ 赞　美　zànměi

Wen Xiaoxi: The first thing that comes to mind is mala when we talk about Sichuan food. Is every Sichuan food tingling and spicy?

Jiang Yihua: I suppose there are also some non-spicy foods, but not that many.

Da Meng: Sichuan cuisine is called a cuisine of "one hundred dishes, one hundred flavors"; there are many kinds of flavors. Apart from mala, there are also hot and sour, hot and sweet, yuxiang, guaiwei and so on.

Jiang Yihua: Is it bothersome to cook Sichuan food?

Da Meng: It's not. The vast majority of Sichuan food is easy to prepare and to learn.

Part 1 【 The Classic: Mala】

Wen Xiaoxi: Yihua, yesterday I had a dish that had it all: hot and tingling, pleasant to both taste buds and eyes!

Jiang Yihua: Really? What dish would be that special?

Wen Xiaoxi: Chilis and chicken. It is made by stir-frying red dried chili pepper, Sichuan pepper and chicken together. The full red chili peppers looked particularly beautiful.

Jiang Yihua: I used not to eat spicy food, but I've come to like it. The Sichuanese are really something else! Combining both the hot and tingling sensations into such a delightful flavor!

Da Meng: Mala is the most special flavor Sichuan cuisine has to offer. While there are some nonlocals that are not a fan of mala, there are also many nonlocals who have fallen in love with this flavor and have taken it back to their hometowns.

Wen Xiaoxi: Isn't that the truth! I like mala so much; I sent some mala spices to my family. My mum likes it!

Jiang Yihua: Da Meng, what are other hot and tingling dishes of Sichuan cuisine? Tell us about them, would you?

Da Meng: There are quite a few of them, for example twice-cooked pork, mapo tofu and boiled fish.

Wen Xiaoxi: Boiled fish? That doesn't sound spicy at all!

Da Meng: If you take its name at face value, it doesn't. In fact, the mala flavor is strong with this one; eating it might make you cry. Nowadays, Sichuan cuisine features a lot of these boiled dishes, for example, boiled beef and boiled sliced meat.

Twice-Cooked Pork

One might call twice-cooked pork the "King of Sichuan Cuisine": it is a home-style dish that is not particularly mala. In Sichuan, almost every household knows the recipe and the dish is universally liked. Simply put, cooked "twice" means putting the already boiled meat back into the pan for stir-frying. Why go through all the trouble? Sichuan people used to offer cooked streaky pork as sacrifice to the gods or ancestors every month. After the act, they were reluctant to waste this meat that was considered "eaten" by the gods and ancestors. Therefore, the Sichuanese sliced the meat and put it back in the pan to stir-fry it, which gave the dish its name "twice-cooked pork". The preparation method may be simple, but the dish is called "King of Sichuan Cuisine" and can be surely found at every Sichuan eatery. It is a dish liked by every Sichuanese.

ma: ★ ★ ★   spiciness: ★ ★ ★

Mapo Tofu

Mapo tofu is another signature dish of Sichuan cuisine and goes back 150 years. At that time, there was a small restaurant at the side of Chengdu's Wanfu Bridge. The owner's second name was Chen, and since her face had a lot of pockmarks, she was called "Chen Pock-Marked Ma". She was the most skilled at preparing tofu: she would braise tofu, minced meat, chili and Sichuan peppers, and chili bean paste together. The result was amazingly tasty and universally liked. Since this dish is both ma and spicy and the owner was called Chen Ma Po, it was called "Mapo Tofu".

ma: ★ ★ ★ ★ ★   spiciness: ★ ★ ★ ★

Part 2 【 Spice and Its Combination With Other Flavors 】

Jiang Yihua: The Sichuanese can really handle spicy food.

Wen Xiaoxi: Well, if they couldn't, they wouldn't be called spicy girls.

Da Meng: The spicy girls love eating hot food, so they create different kinds of hot flavors.

Wen Xiaoxi: Different kinds? What do you mean ?

Da Meng: Many nonlocals assume that Sichuan cuisine only has the mala flavor; in fact, there are many variations: hot and sour, hot and sweet, yuxiang and so on.

Jiang Yihua: Hot and sour? Is this done with vinegar and chili peppers?

Da Meng: That is indeed what some places use, but the classic Sichuanese hot and sour dish is "sliced fish with pickled cabbage", which is made from pickled cabbage and pickled pepper. It is both sour and hot.

Wen Xiaoxi: I know about hot and sweet; that's the flavor of kung pao chicken. What about yuxiang, though?

Da Meng: Yuxiang is a flavor type unique to Sichuan cuisine. "Yuxiang shredded pork" is an incredibly famous dish.

Kung Pao Chicken

Once there lived an official named Ding Baozhen in Sichuan. Ding Baozhen was a foodie. He not only liked going to various regions to eat their specialties, he also often invented recipes. He loved eating chicken and peanuts and especially enjoyed spicy food. He stir-fried chicken, red chili peppers and peanuts together and the result tasted amazing. Later in life, Ding Baozhen became a palace guard (gong bao) and everyone called him Ding Gong Bao and his invention "Gong Bao Ji Ding". After Ding's death, his dish was offered to the emperor by officials and became one of the most famous dishes for consumption by the emperor.

Nowadays, kung pao chicken is considered one of Sichuan's home-style dishes. Since its sweetness has a tone of spiciness and the spiciness a hint of sweetness, it has gained widespread popularity.

sweetness： ★   spiciness： ★ ★

Fish-Flavored Pork

Most eating this dish for their first time have the same question: why is there no fish in fish-flavored pork? If you have the same question, that only means you have been misled by the name. "Fish flavor" is a flavor typical of Sichuan cuisine.

"Fish-flavored" dishes do not contain fish and do not taste like fish; they are merely prepared like fish. Somebody once cooked fish and prepared too much seasoning, which they were reluctant to just throw away. So they used seasoning and stir-fried shredded pork, not expecting it to be as tasty as it was. Later, more and more people stir-fried shredded pork in the same manner and gave the dish a new name: fish-flavored shredded pork.

"Fish-flavored shredded pork" is a dish fried with shredded pork, pickled peppers, green Chinese onion, sugar, vinegar and other condiments. What type of flavor is "fish flavor" exactly?

sweetness: ★ ★   sourness: ★ ★   spiciness: ★

Part 3 【 A Strange Flavor 】

In Sichuan cuisine, you will find a dish called "chicken of strange flavor". Before eating this dish, many are really curious what type of taste might be called "strange". After eating, they struggle to describe what "strange flavor" tastes like.

Talking about flavors, most think of ma, hot, salty, sweet, sour and so on. As foodies, the Sichuanese are above these simple flavors. Resourceful as they are, they found the balancing point of ma, hot, salty, sweet and sour and put them together. It sounds weird but tastes unexpectedly delicious. They call this flavor "strange".

Strange flavor appeared about 70 years ago. The first instance was Chongqing's "broad bean of strange flavor", which became famous. Later on, this type of flavor slowly turned into one of the special flavors found in Sichuan cuisine. The book "Sichuan's Strange Flavor Dishes" gives an overview of 200 strange flavor dishes. Their recipes differ greatly, but they all taste "strange" .

Strangeness: ★ ★ ★ ★ ★

Part 4 【 Chili-less Sichuan Food 】

Wen Xiaoxi: You need to have eaten Sichuan food to know that chilis are amazingly delicious.

Jiang Yihua: And they go so perfectly together with other flavors! They really are a delicacy.

Wen Xiaoxi: Before coming to Sichuan, I thought that I wouldn't survive eating spicy food every day. Now I think that I wouldn't survive not eating spicy.

Jiang Yihua: (Laughter) You can't do without chilis! You've really become a Sichuanese.

Da Meng: Like many non-locals, you two feel that the Sichuanese just can't do without spicy food, but that's not the case. The vast majority of Sichuanese do like eating hot food and are able to prepare great-tasting spicy dishes, but they don't only know how to make this kind of food. They also can do without chilis.

Wen Xiaoxi: Seriously? Is there also chili-less Sichuan food?

Da Meng: Of course there is! Take "sweet and sour spareribs" for example. Its intense sweet-sourness is loved by people of all kinds and ages. Another example is Meishan's beauty food "Dongpo pork shoulder". There is also "fried pork", consisting of streaked pork and salted-and-sun-dried Chinese cabbage.

Dongpo Pork Shoulder

Su Dongpo, Northern Song Dynasty writer, was a gourmet. It is said that the inventor of Dongpo pork shoulder is not Su Dongpo himself, but his wife Wang Fu, who came from Meishan. Once when Wang Fu was stewing pork shoulder, she accidently let the water entirely boil away and the pork shoulder got burnt a bit. In order to cover the burnt flavor, she added a lot of seasoning and carefully boiled the shoulder again. Unexpectedly, Su Dongpo praised this shoulder burnt yellow. Later on, the recipe spread and "Dongpo pork shoulder" became one of Sichuan's signature dishes.

词语

| 神 | shén
god; deity |
| 官 员 | guānyuán
official |

chēng 称	call
bǎi cài bǎi wèi 百 菜 百 味	one hundred dishes, a lot of different flavor
lì hɑi 厉 害	great; impressive; awesome; amazing
wài dì rén 外 地 人	outlander
zhòng 重	heavy

bǐ rú 比 如	for example
dà duō shù 大 多 数	vast majority
dā pèi 搭 配	pair up; match
jiā xiāng 家 乡	hometown; native place
shǔ yú 属 于	belong to; be part of

jì sì	offer sacrifices
祭 祀	(to gods or ancestors)

shě bu de	hate to part with;
舍 不 得	reluctant to do sth.

làng fèi	waste
浪 费	

zǔ xiān	ancestor
祖 先	

piàn	slice
片	

dào	measure word for courses in a meal
道	

láo bǎn niáng	female boss; female shop-owner
老 板 娘	

má zi	pockmark
麻 子	

ná shǒu	adapt; expert; good at
拿 手	

mò	(by grinding) powder; dust; here: grounded meat; minced meat
末	

shāo	braise
烧	

zǔ hé	combination
组 合	

cù	vinegar
醋	

jīng diǎn	classic
经 典	

suān	sour
酸	

yǎn gài	cover (up); conceal
掩 盖	

fā míng 发 明	invent
xiàn 献	offer
yí wèn 疑 问	question
dào dǐ 到 底	on earth
hào qí 好 奇	curious
mǎn zú yú 满 足 于	be content/ satisfied with
què 却	but; yet; however
dà gài 大 概	approximately; about; roughly

gè dì 各 地	various regions; every regions; in all parts of (a country)
qù shì 去 世	die; pass away
yù 御	of an emperor; imperial
chǎo 炒	stir-fry
guài 怪	strange; odd
zuò wéi 作 为	as (in the capacity of)
pínghéngdiǎn 平 衡 点	balancing/ equilibrium point
yì wài 意 外	unexpected

jié hé 结 合	combine; unite
nán nǚ lǎo shào 男 女 老 少	men, women, young and old; everyone; all kinds of people; people of all ages
wén xué jiā 文 学 家	writer; man of letters; literati
dùn 炖	stew
jiāo 焦	burn; char
zàn měi 赞 美	praise

wán měi 完 美	perfect
huó 活	live
měi róng 美 容	improve one's looks; beauty treatment; beautify
měi shí jiā 美 食 家	gourmet
gān 干	dry

专有名词

1. 麻婆豆腐 / Mápó Dòufu / mapo tofu; pockmarked grandma's beancurd; stir-fried beancurd in chili sauce

2. 万福桥 / Wànfú Qiáo / Wanfu Bridge

3. 丁宝桢 / Dīng Bǎozhēn / Ding Baozhen

4. 东坡肘子 / Dōngpō Zhǒuzi / Dongpo pork shoulder

5. 眉山 / Méishān / Meishan

6. 苏东坡 / Sū Dōngpō / Su Dongpo

7. 北宋 / Běi Sòng / Northern Song Dynasty

8. 王弗 / Wáng Fú / Wang Fu

语 言 点

1. 一……就……
2. 被
3. 除了……以外，还……
4. 是……的
5. 把……V.+ 成
6. 虽然……但是……
7. 家家
8. 人人
9. 如果……就……
10. 不过
11. 不仅……而且……
12. 如果……那么……
13. 因……而……
14. 只有……才……
15. 不是……而是……

思 考

1. 你喜欢麻辣吗？你最喜欢哪一个麻辣味的菜？

2. 请你描述一下"麻"是一种什么样的感觉。

3. 除了麻婆豆腐，你还知道哪些川菜的故事？请介绍一下。

4. 请查阅资料或者问中国朋友，川菜里的哪些菜是属于酸辣、甜辣、鱼香味儿的。

5. 除了麻辣、酸辣、甜辣、鱼香，川菜还有些什么味道？

6. 你吃过川菜的"怪味"吗？是什么样的味道？请尽可能描述一下。

7. 你的家乡菜里有没有"怪味"？为什么怪？

8. 川菜的味道是多种多样的，麻辣酸甜都有，请你说出至少五种没有辣椒的川菜名字，并选择其中一种介绍给你的朋友。

第三课 【记忆里的小吃】
Lesson 3 【Childhood Snacks】

【一】那些辣的小吃

文 小西：

　　我喜欢吃辣，大萌，你快介绍一些辣味儿的四川小吃吧。

大 萌：

　　辣味儿的小吃有很多，比如钟水饺就是很有名的四川小吃。

文 小西：

　　钟水饺？水饺不是北方的食物吗？怎么成了四川小吃？

大 萌：

　　四川的钟水饺跟北方的水饺不一样。北方的水饺馅儿里一般都有菜，但是钟水饺是纯肉馅儿的，而且钟水饺的红辣椒油也很特别，酱也很香。

文 小西：

　　红红的辣椒油、香香的酱、纯肉馅儿……我要流口水了。

大 萌：

　　哈哈，这就流口水了？四川的"担担面"，一碗面里就有二十几种调料。还有让你辣到哭，哭完还要接着吃的"伤心凉粉"。

① 钟水饺　　Zhōng Shuǐjiǎo
② 食 物　　shíwù
③ 馅 儿　　xiànr
④ 纯　　　 chún
⑤ 流　　　 liú
⑥ 口 水　　kǒushuǐ
⑦ 担担面　 Dàndan Miàn
⑧ 接 着　　jiēzhe
⑨ 伤心凉粉
　　Shāngxīn Liángfěn

伤心凉粉

① 清　朝　Qīng Cháo
② 豌　豆　wāndòu
③ 口　感　kǒugǎn
④ 以　上　yǐshàng
⑤ 其　中　qízhōng
⑥ 泪　　　lèi

　　伤心凉粉起源于清朝（1616—1911年），是百年名小吃。这种凉粉是用豌豆做的黄凉粉，口感跟一般的白凉粉不同。伤心凉粉的特点就是它的调料，一碗伤心凉粉大概有13种以上的调料，其中最主要的就是特辣辣椒油。伤心凉粉有多辣？不太能吃辣的人要喝一口水吃一口凉粉，而喜欢吃辣的四川人也会被辣得流泪，不知道的人就会以为是因为吃凉粉的时候想到伤心的事所以流泪。一边吃一边流泪的人多了，凉粉就有了新的名字——伤心凉粉。

　　虽然伤心凉粉让人辣得"伤心"，但是吃货们只要吃过一次，就再也停不下来了。

麻：★ ★ ★　　　辣：★ ★ ★ ★ ★

【二】小吃也很甜

文小西：
　四川人的爱好太特别了，连小吃都可以这么辣。我家乡的小吃，大多数都是甜的。

大萌：
　四川也有甜的小吃啊。比如四川名小吃"赖汤圆"就是甜的。

文小西：

　　赖汤圆？汤圆有什么特别的呢？

大萌：

　　卖汤圆的老板姓赖，所以大家叫他的汤圆为"赖汤圆"。赖汤圆的特点是"煮时不浑汤，吃时三不沾①"。经过一百多年的发展，赖汤圆现在有十几种不同的馅儿，而且不同馅儿的汤圆还做成了不同的样子，非常漂亮。

文小西：

　　真是又好吃又好看啊。

大萌：

　　四川小吃里还有一种只属于夏天的小吃。

文小西：

　　小吃也有季节？

大萌：

　　是的，这就是"凉糕"。

文小西：

　　名字听起来很舒服，它是用什么做的？

① 赖汤圆　Lài Tāngyuán
② 发展　fāzhǎn
③ 凉糕　liánggāo
④ 冷藏　lěngcáng
⑤ 红糖　hóngtáng
⑥ 错过　cuòguò

① 三不沾：不沾筷、不沾碗、不沾牙。表示汤圆的选料好，糯米粉磨得好，而且揉得也很好。

大 萌：

用米做的，做好以后放在冰箱里冷藏，吃的时候加上红糖水。在四川夏天三四十度的天气里，吃一碗甜甜的凉糕，非常舒服。夏天来成都旅行的人，一定不能错过凉糕。

【三】小吃里的艺术品

①追 求　zhuīqiú
②执 着　zhízhuó
③艺术性　yìshùxìng
④三大炮　Sāndàpào

文 小西：

四川人对美食的追求真的很执着。

大 萌：

是啊，这些"吃货"们对食物的要求非常高呢，不仅要好吃好看，还要有艺术性。

文 小西：

艺术？小吃和艺术有什么关系？

大 萌：

在四川小吃里就有一些"艺术品"。比如三大炮。

文 小西：

三大炮是什么？

大 萌：

在所有的四川小吃里，三大炮是最特别的一种——有声有味有意思。三大炮有点儿像糍粑，因为做的时候会发出"砰砰砰"三声响，就好像三声大炮的声音，所以把这种小吃叫作"三大炮"。围着看三大炮的人里面，一半是为了吃，一半是为了看热闹、看表演。

文 小西：

这个很有意思，在哪里可以看到三大炮？

大 萌：

三大炮这种小吃一般是表演给游客看的，现在会这种传统工艺的人越来越少。如果想吃三大炮，也只能去宽窄巷子、文殊坊、锦里这三个地方了，其他地方只有在一些特别的时间里才有。

⑤糍粑　cíbā
⑥砰　　pēng
⑦响　　xiǎng
⑧围　　wéi
⑨游客　yóukè
⑩工艺　gōngyì
⑪宽窄巷子
　Kuān Zhǎi Xiàngzi
⑫文殊坊
　Wén Shū Fāng
⑬锦里　Jǐnlǐ

甜：★★★　艺术性：★★

① 糖 画　tánghuà
② 景 点　jǐngdiǎn
③ 摊　tān
④ 艺 人　yìrén
⑤ 据 说　jùshuō
⑥ 诗　shī
⑦ 陈子昂　Chén Zǐáng
⑧ 皇 帝　huángdì
⑨ 魅 力　mèilì
⑩ 世 家　shìjiā
⑪ 蔡树全　Cài Shùquán
⑫ 联合国教科文组织
　　Liánhéguó Jiàokēwén Zǔzhī
⑬ 授 予　shòuyǔ
⑭ 称 号　chēnghào

糖 画

　　糖画，就是用糖做的画。在四川的很多旅游景点都会看到糖画小摊，你想要什么画，糖画艺人就能用糖给你画出来。

　　据说最早做糖画的是四川诗人陈子昂，他做的糖画又好吃又好看。后来，皇帝知道了，非常喜欢，就常常让陈子昂做糖画。38岁那年，陈子昂回到四川，开始教大家做糖画。现在做糖画的艺人越来越少，但是糖画的魅力没有减少。出生于四川糖画世家的蔡树全就在国内外很多地方表演过糖画，更被联合国教科文组织授予"一级民间工艺美术家"的称号。

甜：★★★★★　艺术性：★★★★

Part 1 【 Those Spicy Snacks 】

Wen Xiaoxi: I like eating spicy. Da Meng, would you please introduce us some spicy Sichuan snacks in no time?

Da Meng: There are lots of spicy snacks, for example, bell dumplings, which are a famous Sichuan snack.

Wen Xiaoxi: Bell dumplings? Aren't those boiled? Don't boiled dumplings come from the North of China? How come they turned into a Sichuanese snack?

Da Meng: Bell dumplings and the boiled dumplings from the North are not alike. The Northern dumplings usually have vegetable stuffing, but bell dumplings have pure meat stuffing. They are eaten with red chili oil, which is special by itself, and fragrant soy sauce.

Wen Xiaoxi: Full red chili oil, fragrant soy sauce, pure meat stuffing… I'm about to drool!

Da Meng: (Laughing) So fast already? Have some of Sichuan's "Dandan noodles"; one bowl has more than 20 kinds of flavorings. It's so hot that it'll make you cry! After you're done crying, you'll eat some sad jelly noodles.

Sad Jelly Noodles

The sad jelly noodles came about in the Qing Dynasty (1616—1911) and have been famous for over a hundred years. The noodles are made from peas turned into a yellow jelly, making their texture feel different when compared with white jelly. What makes sad jelly noodles so special is their seasoning, of which a bowl has more than 13, with the most important being extra spicy chili oil. How spicy, you might ask? Those not at all apt at eating spicy drink a sip of water with every bite of jelly, while even the spice-loving Sichuanese feel the heat so much so that they shed tears. Outsiders might assume that thinking of something sad while eating these jelly noodles makes you weep. As more and more people cried while eating this dish, these jelly noodles got a new name: sad jelly noodles.

Sad jelly noodles are so spicy that they make you "sad", but once foodies dig in for their first time, they do not want to stop.

ma: ★★★   spiciness: ★★★★★

Part2 【Snacks, Oh So Sweet! 】

Wen Xiaoxi: Sichuanese people's appetite is really something else, even their snacks are incredibly spicy. Most of my hometown snacks are sweet.

Da Meng: Sichuan also has sweet snacks! Take the famous "Lai's Glutinous Rice Balls (Lai tangyuan)" as an example.

Wen Xiaoxi: Lai's Glutinous Rice Balls? What's special about them?

Da Meng: A restaurant owner named Lai sold tangyuan, so everyone called his tangyuan "Lai's Tangyuan". They're special because "during boiling, they do not make the soup go cloudy; during eating, they do not stick everywhere"①. Undergoing refinement for more than a hundred years, lai tangyuan now comes with a dozen different fillings. What's more, differently filled tangyuan also come in different shapes. They're so pretty!

Wen Xiaoxi: So, both delicious and good-looking!

Da Meng: There is also a snack only eaten during summer.

Wen Xiaoxi: There are also seasonal snacks?

Da Meng: There are. In this case, it would be "cold rice cake".

Wen Xiaoxi: I like the sound of this name. How is it prepared?

Da Meng: It is made of rice. After preparation, the cake is kept cold in the fridge, and served with brown sugar syrup. During summer, when it has 30 to 40 degrees Celsius in Sichuan, eating a bowl of sweet cold rice cake is just swell. Those who come to Chengdu during summer can't miss cool rice cake!

① "three non-sticking": does not stick to chopsticks, bowl and teeth, meaning that the ingredients for making tangyuan are well-chosen and that the glutinous rice flour was ground and rubbed well.

Part3 【Artistic Snacks 】

Wen Xiaoxi: The Sichuanese are really dedicated in their pursuit of the fine foods.

Da Meng: You can say that again! These foodies have high standards: not only has food to taste and look good, it also has to be artistic.

Wen Xiaoxi: Artistic? What do snacks and art have in common?

Da Meng: Some Sichuan snacks are "works of art", for example, the "Three Cannonballs" (san da pao).

Wen Xiaoxi: What are the "Three Cannonballs"?

Da Meng: Among all Sichuan snacks, san da pao is the most special: they sound dramatic, taste amazing, and are simply a delight. They're a bit like black sesame rice cake: during preparation, they're thrown against a tray and produce "bang, bang, bang" sounds, just like three cannonballs, which is how they got their name. Among those who watch the preparation of this snack, one half does it for the food, and the other for the fun of it and enjoy the show.

Wen Xiaoxi: How fascinating! Where can we see this show?

Da Meng: It is generally performed for tourists, but there are less and less people who are skilled in this traditional craft. If you want to eat "The Three Cannonballs", your only choice is to go to Kuanzhai Alley, Wenshu Fang and Jinli. Other places only have them on special occasions.

Sugar Paintings

Sugar Paintings are paintings made from sugar. At many tourist attractions in Sichuan, you will see sugar painting stalls. The sugar painting artisan can draw any painting you want.

It is said that the earliest sugar painting was made by Sichuan poet Chen Ziang, and his paintings were both tasty and eye-catching. Later on, the emperor learnt about his paintings and liked them a lot, and often had Chen Ziang make sugar paintings for him. Today, there are fewer and fewer craftsmen who make sugar paintings, but they are as charming as ever. Cai Shuquan, born in an old family of Sichuanese sugar painters, has given performances of his art both domestic and abroad, and was awarded the title of "First-Class Folk Artist" by UNESCO.

sweetness: ★★★★★   artistry: ★★★★★

词 语

天 堂	tiān táng paradise	口 水	kóu shuǐ saliva	皇 帝	huáng dì emperor

xián 闲	not in use; unoccupied; idle	shí wù 食 物	food
xiànr 馅儿	filling; stuffing	chún 纯	pure
liú 流	flow	jiē zhe 接 着	after that; subsequently
kǒu gǎn 口 感	texture (of foods)	yǐ shàng 以 上	(of number or quantity) more than…; over; above
qí zhōng 其 中	among them; of them; in it	lèi 泪	tear

fā zhǎn 发 展	development; growth; advance; expand; here: refinement
cuò guò 错 过	miss
zhí zhuó 执 着	persistent; dedicated
pēng 砰	(onom.) bang
wéi 围	surround: all around; encircle
gōng yì 工 艺	craft
tān 摊	vendor's stand; booth; stall; kiosk
jù shuō 据 说	it is said; allegedly

hóng táng 红 糖	brown sugar
zhuī qiú 追 求	seek; pursue
yì shù xìng 艺 术 性	artistic
xiǎng 响	sound: noise
yóu kè 游 客	tourist; visitor
jǐng diǎn 景 点	scenic spot; place of interest; attraction (tourism)
yì rén 艺 人	artisan; handicraftsman; performing artist
shī 诗	poem

mèi lì 魅 力	charm	shì jiā 世 家	prominent old family; aristocratic family
shòu yǔ 授 予	confer; award	chēng hào 称 号	title

专 有 名 词

1. 钟水饺 / Zhōng Shuǐjiǎo / bell dumplings

2. 担担面 / Dàndan Miàn / dandan noodles

3. 伤心凉粉 / Shāngxīn Liángfěn / sad (pea) jelly noodles

4. 清朝 / Qīng Cháo / Qing Dynasty

5. 赖汤圆 / Lài Tāngyuán / (Mr.) Lai's Glutinous Rice Balls; Lai Tang Yuan

6. 三大炮 / Sāndà Pào / san da pao; The Three Cannonballs

7. 宽窄巷子 / Kuān Zhǎi Xiàngzǐ / Kuanzhai Alley

8. 文殊坊 / Wénshū Fāng / Wenshufang

9. 锦里 / Jǐnlǐ / Jinli

10. 陈子昂 / Chén Zǐáng / Chen Ziang

11. 蔡树全 / Cài Shùquán / Cai Shuquan

12. 联合国教科文组织 / Liánhéguó Jiào Kē Wén Zǔzhī / UNESCO

语言点

1. 既然……那么……

2. 只要……就……

3. 连……都……

思考

1. 你吃过四川小吃吗？辣味儿的四川小吃里，给你印象最深刻的是哪一种？为什么？

2. 你吃过糖画和三大炮吗？你觉得怎么样？

3. 你家乡小吃里，有像糖画和三大炮一样有艺术性的小吃吗？请举例说明。

第四课
Lesson 4

【 川菜的 "灵魂" 】
【 The "Soul" of Sichuan Cuisine 】

① 灵魂　línghún
② 甚至　shènzhì
③ 伟大　wěidà
④ 创造　chuàngzào

江一华：
四川真是吃货们的天堂啊。

文小西：
对啊。有那么多的川菜，那么多的名小吃，我太爱这里了。

大萌：
我们常说，菜好不好吃，主要看味道；味道好不好，主要看调料。你们知道川菜主要用些什么调料吗？

文小西：
我知道有辣椒，因为川菜很辣。

江一华：
川菜的辣是因为辣椒，川菜的麻是因为花椒。对不对？

大萌：
对。辣椒和花椒是川菜的特色。不过，还有一种调料被称为川菜的灵魂，大多数的川菜都离不开它，这就是"豆瓣酱"。有人甚至说，豆瓣酱是四川人最伟大的创造之一。

【一】辣椒

七千多年前，辣椒在美洲被发现，后来，墨西哥人开始大量种辣椒，可以说，辣椒是人类种植的最古老的农作物之一。

明朝末年，辣椒传到中国。辣椒通过不同的方式进入四川，所以就有了不同的名字。辣椒最早来中国的时候，是从海上来的，所以有的人叫它"海椒"。四川在中国的西南，辣椒除了从海上来到四川以外，还有一些辣椒是通过丝绸之路，从西亚来到陕西，然后从陕西来到四川的，陕西简称"秦"，所以也有一些人叫辣椒为"秦椒"。

四川人喜欢吃辣椒，也喜欢种辣椒。不过最早的辣椒是被当成花来种的，叫作"辣椒花"。后来人们才发现辣椒特别的味道，让辣椒从花变成了调料。现在的辣椒有很多不同的品种，它们的颜色、样子和辣味儿都不一样。比如有一种辣椒长得大大的，像灯笼一样，有的人叫它"灯笼椒"，也有的人叫它"菜椒"，甚至因为不辣，反而有点儿甜，所以有的人叫它"甜椒"。再比如有一种辣椒，细细的、长长的，辣椒的尖朝着天空的方向，我们叫它"朝天椒"。朝天椒的味道辣极了，外地人不太敢吃，四川人却非常喜欢。

在所有的从外国来的香料里，辣椒是来得最晚却使用最多的一种香料。现在的辣椒是川菜里主要的调料之一，辣已经成了川菜的重要特点。

①	美 洲	Měi Zhōu
②	墨西哥	Mò Xī Gē
③	大 量	dàliàng
④	古 老	gǔlǎo
⑤	农作物	nóngzuòwù
⑥	明 朝	Míng Cháo
⑦	方 式	fāngshì
⑧	通 过	tōngguò
⑨	丝绸之路	Sī Chóu Zhī Lù
⑩	西 亚	Xī Yà
⑪	陕 西	Shǎnxī
⑫	简	jiǎn
⑬	品 种	pǐnzhǒng
⑭	灯 笼	dēnglong
⑮	反 而	fǎnér
⑯	细	xì
⑰	尖	jiān
⑱	朝	cháo
⑲	香 料	xiāngliào

【二】花椒

①普 遍	pǔbiàn
②用 处	yòngchù
③肥 皂	féizào
④籽	zǐ
⑤辟 邪	bìxié
⑥西 汉	Xī Hàn
⑦粉	fěn
⑧抹	mǒ
⑨祛 除	qūchú
⑩腥味儿	xīngwèir
⑪唐 朝	Táng Cháo
⑫产 地	chǎndì
⑬汉 源	Hànyuán
⑭茂 县	Màoxiàn
⑮椒麻鸡	Jiāomá Jī
⑯接 受	jiēshòu

川菜的特点是"麻辣"，"麻"是因为有花椒。跟辣椒不同，花椒是中国特有的一种香料，已经有两千多年的历史了。

现在我们普遍认为花椒用处很多——可以做调料，也可以用在中药里，还可以做成肥皂。不过在古时候，花椒的用处不太一样。花椒树的籽很多，香味儿也很浓。很多人会在家门口种一棵花椒树，一方面是希望自己家能跟花椒树一样多子（多籽），另一方面，古时候的人相信花椒的香味儿能辟邪。在一千年前的西汉时期，用花椒的花做成粉，抹在墙上，颜色很漂亮，味道也很香，这样的房子称为"椒房"，当时椒房是皇后住的。在那个时候，花椒是只有皇室才能使用的香料。

做菜的时候加点儿花椒，主要是祛除肉的腥味儿。在没有辣椒的中国古代，花椒是最主要的辣味调料，在唐朝（618—907 年），几乎三分之一的菜里都要放花椒。现在川菜里还在大量用花椒，别的地方的菜已经极少用了。

四川是花椒的主要产地。四川最好的花椒是红花椒，比如汉源和茂县的花椒。红花椒非常麻，主要和辣椒一起用来做一些麻辣味儿很重的菜，比如辣子鸡。另外一种花椒是青花椒。青花椒是一种新品种的花椒，不太麻，主要用来做一些炒菜，比如椒麻鸡等。一般来说，外地人比较喜欢青花椒，现在在川菜里，青花椒用得也越来越多了。

作为一种中国特产，很多外国人不认识花椒，在传统的西餐里也不用花椒，在西方人眼里，花椒就是"四川胡椒"（Sichuan Pepper）。但是来过中国的大多数外国朋友都比较喜欢"麻婆豆腐"这个菜，这是否说明外国人也能接受花椒的味道呢？

【三】豆瓣酱

豆瓣，也叫胡豆瓣。把豆瓣和辣椒一起发酵做成的豆瓣酱，被称为"川菜的灵魂"，已经有三百多年的历史了。四川的豆瓣酱有很多，以郫县豆瓣酱为代表，其中最有名的就是"益丰和"和"鹃城牌"两个品牌了。

豆瓣酱的制作非常麻烦，首先要用最好的二荆条红辣椒跟盐一起在太阳下晒；其次要把胡豆瓣发酵六个月以上，做成甜豆瓣；最后把晒好的辣椒和发酵好的甜豆瓣混合，再放在太阳下晒三个月到一年的时间。这样做出来的豆瓣酱，虽然没有加别的香料，但是颜色却很红，味道也非常香。

都说四川人能吃辣，会吃辣，更会做辣。在川菜的二十三种常用的味道里，跟辣有关的味道就有13种，比如麻辣、香辣、酸辣、甜辣、怪味等。而这些味道都离不开豆瓣酱。豆瓣酱的用法很多，可以在炒菜的时候当成调料加进去，也可以直接当蘸料，还可以放在面条里，增加面条的香味儿。

现在的豆瓣酱已经走出了四川，走向了国际，并且根据大家的口味和要求，在豆瓣酱的基础上生产出了很多新的酱料，比如香菇酱、豆豉酱，还有最近在国外很流行的川香酱等。

① 豆　瓣　dòubàn
② 发　酵　fājiào
③ 郫　县　Pí Xiàn
④ 益丰和　Yì Fēng Hé
⑤ 鹃城牌　Juān Chéng Pái
⑥ 品　牌　pǐnpái
⑦ 制　作　zhìzuò
⑧ 二荆条　Èr Jīng Tiáo
⑨ 晒　　shài
⑩ 混　合　hùnhé
⑪ 增　加　zēngjiā
⑫ 国　际　guójì
⑬ 基　础　jīchǔ

Jiang Yihua: Sichuan really is foodies' paradise.

Wen Xiaoxi: It sure is! So many Sichuanese foods, so many famous snacks, I just love it here!

Da Meng: We often say whether food tastes good or not depends on its flavor; and whether the flavor is any good or not depends on the seasoning used. Do you know what seasonings are mainly used in Sichuan food?

Wen Xiaoxi: I know there are chili peppers, because Sichuan food is hot.

Jiang Yihua: Food here is hot because of chili peppers and ma because of Sichuan pepper, right?

Da Meng: Correct. Chili peppers and Sichuan peppers are specialties of Sichuan cuisine. Having said that, there is another seasoning called the "soul of Sichuan cuisine", which is found in the vast majority of food here: chili bean paste. Some even say that chili bean paste is one of Sichuan's greatest creations.

Part 1 【 Peppers 】

More than 7,000 years ago, peppers were discovered in the Americas. Later, Mexicans began to grow peppers in large quantities. One could argue that peppers are one of the oldest crops grown by people.

During the Late Ming Dynasty, peppers made their way to China. They arrived through differing means in Sichuan, so they had differing names. Peppers first came to China through the sea, so some called them "Hai Jiao". As Sichuan is situated in China's Southwest, some peppers, apart from the ones from the sea, also made their way there through the silk road. They came from West Asia and arrived in Shaanxi, and then from Shaanxi to Sichuan. Shaanxi's short name is "Qin", so there were some who called these peppers "Qin peppers".

The Sichuanese not only like eating peppers, they also like cultivating them. The earliest peppers were cultivated as flowers, though, and called "pepper flowers". Later, their special flavor was discovered, and they were no longer treated as flowers, but as seasoning. Today, there are various varieties of peppers with differing colors, shape and spiciness. For example, one variety grows really big into what looks like a bell, so some call them "Lantern-shaped peppers" and some also call them "Dish peppers", which some other people even call "sweet peppers" owing to their sweet tastes.There's another variety of pepper growing long and thin, with its tip pointing upwards towards the sky, which is called "Facing heaven pepper". They are extremely hot. Nonlocals don't dare to eat them, while the Sichuanese love them.

Among all the spices coming from abroad, peppers arrived the latest but are used the most. Today, they are the main seasoning used in Sichuan cuisine and have become its important characteristic.

Part 2 【 Sichuan Pepper 】

Sichuan cuisine is characterized by "hot and numbing". The numbing sensation is caused by Sichuan pepper. It is different from chili peppers and is a spice unique to China. It goes back more than 2,000 years in time.

Nowadays, we generally think that Sichuan pepper has a lot of applications: as seasoning, in traditional Chinese medicine, or as soap. In ancient China, though, the applications were quite different. Sichuan pepper trees have a lot of seeds and their fragrance is intense. A lot of people used to plant a Sichuan pepper tree at their front door; on the one hand, in the hope that their own family may have as many sons as the tree has seeds, on the other hand, in the belief that the fragrance will ward off evil. During the Western Han Dynasty one thousand years ago, people used to take the flowers of Sichuan pepper trees and ground them into powder, which they plastered onto walls. This gave the walls a pretty color and a fragrant smell. These houses were called "Pepper Houses". At that time, these pepper houses were occupied by the Empress. Sichuan pepper was a spice only the imperial family could use.

Adding Sichuan pepper during cooking was mainly done to get rid of the foul smell of meat. As chili peppers did not exist in ancient China, Sichuan pepper was the main pungent condiment: In the Tang Dynasty (618-907 AD), Sichuan pepper was used in almost one third of all dishes. Today, Sichuan cuisine still uses a large amount of this pepper, while its usage elsewhere has greatly gone back.

Sichuan is the main source of Sichuan pepper, with the best variety being the red Sichuan pepper, which can be found in Hanyuan and Mao County, for example. Red Sichuan pepper is incredibly numbing and is mainly used together with chili peppers for the preparation of some extremely mala.

As a Chinese specialty, many people from abroad do not know Sichuan pepper, which is why in English it is named after its source of production: Sichuan.Having said that, most foreign friends who have been to China rather like "Mapo Tofu". Does this not mean that people from other countries can also accept the numbing flavor of Sichuan pepper?

Part 3 【 Chili Bean Paste 】

Broad beans, or fava beans, ferment together with chili peppers and result in chili bean paste, which is called the soul of Sichuan cuisine, and has a history of more than 300 years. There is a broad range of chili bean pastes, with Pixian doubanjiang being the figurehead. Their most famous brands are Yifenghe and Juancheng Pai.

Chili bean paste production is very tricky. First, the best erjingtiao red chili pepper is dried in the sun together with salt. Second, the bean paste has to ferment for more than half a year to turn into sweet bean paste. Last, the dried peppers and the fermented bean paste are mixed and placed in sunlight again to dry for three to twelve months. Chili bean paste that is produced in this fashion is bright red and has a fragrant taste, although no other spices are added.

We all know that the Sichuanese eat and, most importantly, prepare their spicy foods. In the commonly used 23 flavors of Sichuan cuisine, 13 of them are hot, for example, hot and numbing, hot and fragrant, hot and sour, hot and sweet, guaiwei and so on. These flavors can't do without chili bean paste. There are lots of applications for this paste: it can be used as cooking seasoning, directly as a dip, or put in noodles dishes to give them a more fragrant flavor.

Today, chili bean paste has gone international. What is more, because of differing tastes and demands, a lot of new sauces have been produced on the basis of chili bean paste, such as mushroom sauce, fermented black soybean sauce as well as the chuanxiang sauce, which has recently become popular abroad.

| 词 | 语 |

| 灵 魂 | línghún
soul |  农 作 物 | nóngzuòwù
crops |  抹 | mǒ
apply; smear; plaster |

shèn zhì 甚 至	even; (go) so far as to; so much so that	wěi dà 伟 大	great; grand
chuàng zào 创 造	create	dà liàng 大 量	large in number or quantity
fāng shì 方 式	way; fashion; pattern	tōng guò 通 过	through
jiǎn 简	simple; brief	pǐn zhǒng 品 种	variety
dēng long 灯 笼	lantern	fǎn ér 反 而	on the contrary; instead
xì 细	thin	jiān 尖	point; tip

xiāng liào 香 料	spice; flavoring; condiment	
yòng chù 用 处	use	
bì xié 辟 邪	ward off evil spirits	
féi zào 肥 皂	soap	
xīng wèir 腥味儿	foul smell (of fish or meat)	
chǎn dì 产 地	place of production (or origin)	
fā jiào 发 酵	ferment	
shài 晒	dry in the sun	

pǔ biàn 普 遍	universal; general
zǐ 籽	seed
fěn 粉	powder
qū chú 祛 除	dispel; get rid of
jiē shòu 接 受	accept
pǐn pái 品 牌	brand
zhì zuò 制 作	make; manufacture
hùn hé 混 合	mix; blend

zēng jiā 增 加	increase
jī chǔ 基 础	foundation; basis; base

guó jì 国 际	international

专 有 名 词

1. 美洲   / Měizhōu / America; the Americas; American continent

2. 汉源   / Hànyuán / Hanyuan County

3. 墨西哥   / Mò Xī Gē / Mexico

4. 茂县   / Mào Xiàn / Maoxian County

5. 明朝   / Míng Cháo / Ming Dynasty

6. 丝绸之路   / Sī Chóu Zhī Lù / Silk Road

7. 西亚   / xī yà / West Asia

8. 郫县   / PíXiàn / Pixian County

9. 陕西   / Shǎn Xī / Shaanxi

10. 益丰和   / Yì Fēng Hé / Yifenghe

11. 西汉   / Xī Hàn / Western Han Dynasty (206BC-25AD)

12. 鹃城牌   / Juānchéng Pái / Juanchengpai

13. 唐朝   / Táng Cháo / Tang Dynasty

14. 二荆条   / Er Jīng Tiáo / Erjingtiao

语 言 点

一方面……，另一方面……

思 考

1. 请比较中国不同地方的辣都有什么不一样。
2. 你的家乡菜里有豆瓣酱这样的"灵魂调料"吗？
请介绍一下。

第五课 【川菜博物馆】
Lesson 5 【Sichuan Cuisine Museum】

大 萌：

你们知道吗？成都有一个川菜博物馆。

文 小西：

川菜还有博物馆？

大 萌：

是的，成都的川菜博物馆是世界上唯一以菜文化为内容的博物馆。

文 小西：

真有意思，第一次听说菜文化的博物馆。川菜博物馆里有些什么？

大 萌：

川菜博物馆里分典藏馆、互动演示馆、品茗休闲馆等。典藏馆里有很多有关川菜的书和图片，我们可以在这里了解川菜的历史和文化。互动演示馆里可以互动，我们既可以看川菜师傅们做川菜，也可以参与互动，自己做川菜。

文 小西：

还能自己做川菜？很有意思。

① 唯一　wéiyī
② 内容　nèiróng
③ 典藏馆　diǎncáng guǎn
④ 互动演示馆
　　hùdòng yǎnshì guǎn
⑤ 品茗休闲馆
　　pǐnmíng xiūxián guǎn
⑥ 参与　cānyù
⑦ 茶饭相随、饮食相依
　　chá fàn xiāng suí、
　　　yǐn shí xiāng yī

⑧方　面　fāngmiàn
⑨坝坝茶　bà ba chá

江一华：

"茗"是茶的意思吧？为什么川菜博物馆里还有茶？

大　萌：

这是川菜文化里"茶饭相随、饮食相依"的特点。喝茶是四川人生活的重要方面。春天和秋天天气很好，四川人喜欢一边晒着太阳一边喝"坝坝茶"；夏天有点儿热的时候，四川人喜欢在树下喝"林荫茶"；冬天很冷，四川人会到茶馆喝茶。不管是哪一种形式的茶，游客都可以在品茗休闲馆里体验到。

Da Meng: Did you know Chengdu has a Sichuan Cuisine Museum?

Jiang Yihua: A museum just for Sichuan food?

Da Meng: Yes. The Sichuan Cuisine Museum in Chengdu is the world's only museum that exhibits food culture.

Wen Xiaoxi: Fascinating! That's the first time I've heard of a food culture museum. What can you see?

Da Meng: The museum is divided into several halls: Classical Collection, Interactive Demonstration, Tea Service & Leisure, and many more. In the Classical Collection Hall are a lot of books and pictures of Sichuan cuisine; we can learn more about the history and culture of Sichuan food. In the Interactive Demonstration Hall, we can watch Sichuanese chefs prepare Sichuan food and we can also participate and interact with them, and make Sichuan food ourselves.

Wen Xiaoxi: Make Sichuan food ourselves? Wow!

Jiang Yihua: How come there is a tea hall?

Da Meng: This is a characteristic of Sichuan food culture: "Tea and rice go together; food and drink rely on each other." Drinking tea is an important aspect of life in Sichuan. In spring and autumn, when the weather's nice, the Sichuanese like basking in the sun and sip some "baba tea". When it's hot in summer, they like drinking "linyin tea" in the shade of a tree. It's cold in winter and that's when the Sichuanese go to teahouses to drink their tea. No matter what kind of tea, tourists can experience them all in the Tea Service & Leisure Hall.

词 语

林 荫　línyīn
tree shade

体 验　tǐyàn
experience for oneself

wéi yī 唯 一	only; sole		nèi róng 内 容	content
cān yù 参 与	participate in; have a hand in		fāng miàn 方 面	aspect

chá fàn xiāng suí　yǐn shí xiāng yī
茶 饭 相 随、饮 食 相 依

Tea and rice go together;
food and drink rely on each other.

语言点

不管……都……

思考

1. 请查阅资料，了解一下川菜博物馆的具体情况，把你了解到的情况在班里跟别的同学分享一下。

2. 川菜文化里的"茶饭相随、饮食相依"是什么意思？请举例说明。

第六课
Lesson 6 　【随季节变化的川菜】
　【Seasonal Sichuan Food】

【一】节日里的菜

① 部　　　　bù
② 剩　　　　shèng
③ 年年有余　niánnián yǒuyú
④ 春 节　　　Chūn Jié
⑤ 团团圆圆　tuántuán yuányuán
⑥ 幸 福　　　xìngfú
⑦ 中秋节　　Zhōngqiū Jié
⑧ 黏　　　　nián
⑨ 月 饼　　　yuèbǐng
⑩ 传 统　　　chuántǒng
⑪ 战 争　　　zhànzhēng
⑫ 平平安安　píngpíng ānān
⑬ 观 念　　　guānniàn

江一华：

昨天我看了一部电影，电影里的中国人在春节的时候吃鱼，吃一半剩一半。大萌，你知道为什么这样吗？

大萌：

因为想要"年年有余"嘛。

文小西：

年年有余是什么意思？

大萌：

今年有鱼吃，没吃完，剩下的明年吃，所以是"年年有鱼"，这个词的发音跟"年年有余"一样。人们希望自己的生活越来越好，每年都有剩的，所以每年春节都要说"年年有鱼（余）"。

文小西：

挺有意思的，还有别的吗？

大萌：

有很多，比如春节的时候吃汤圆，汤圆是圆的，是希望一家人像汤圆一样团团圆圆；汤圆是甜的，是希望一家人的生活能像汤圆一样甜、一样幸福。比如中秋节吃糍粑，糍粑像中秋节的月亮一样又大又圆，也是希望一家人能像糍粑一样团团圆圆；糍粑是糯米做的，很甜很黏，是希望吃了糍粑以后，能把一家人黏在一起，不要分开。

江一华：

中秋节不是吃月饼吗？

大萌：

对，北方人中秋节吃月饼，四川人中秋节的传统是吃糍粑，不过现在也有很多四川人中秋节那天吃月饼。

文小西：

为什么中国人这么喜欢团圆？

大萌：

因为以前常常有战争，人们觉得，一家人能平平安安地在一起，就是最大的幸福。现在虽然没有战争了，但是"团圆"已经成了中国的传统家庭观念之一了。

【二】24 节气里的川菜

文小西：

我想吃月饼了，我们去买点儿吧。

大 萌：

现在不是吃月饼的时间，买不到吧。

文小西：

什么意思？

大 萌：

孔子说过"不时不食"，意思就是"不是这个季节的东西不能吃"。

文小西：

为什么不能吃？

大 萌：

因为不同季节的食物不一样。比如说，西红柿是夏天的食物，7 月的西红柿比 1 月的西红柿多一倍的维生素 C。菠菜是冬天的食物，冬天的菠菜比夏天的菠菜多 8 倍的营养。

文 小西：

我懂了。以后吃饭的时候，我也要"不时不食"。

大 萌：

除了不同季节的食物不一样以外，中医认为，人的身体和季节也有很大关系。不同季节的天气不一样，人们身体需要的也不一样，所以应该吃不一样的食物。

①	按照	ànzhào
②	节气	jiéqì
③	立春	Lì Chūn
④	嫩	nèn
⑤	芽	yá
⑥	春卷	chūnjuǎn
⑦	庆祝	qìngzhù
⑧	雨水	Yǔ Shuǐ
⑨	清明	Qīng Míng
⑩	清明菜	Qīng Míng Cài
⑪	粑粑	bā bā
⑫	冬至	Dōng Zhì
⑬	小寒	Xiǎo Hán
⑭	八宝粥	Bā Bǎo Zhōu
⑮	保暖	bǎonuǎn

中国人按照天气的变化，把一年的时间分成二十四个节气。立春是二十四节气里的第一个节气，立春以后冬天很快就要过去，春天很快就要来临，白天的时间越来越长，太阳越来越暖和，蔬菜也开始长出嫩芽。立春这一天用蔬菜的嫩芽做成春卷，庆祝春天的到来；把春卷送给朋友们吃，希望第二年大家都会得到更多的食物。雨水的时候四川人要吃罐罐肉；清明要吃清明菜，做清明菜粑粑（四川话）；冬至的时候吃了羊肉，一个冬天都不会觉得冷；小寒是一年里最冷的一天，这一天应该吃八宝粥，能更好地保暖。

Part 1 【Festive Food】

Jiang Yihua: I saw a movie yesterday. The Chinese in the movie had fish during the spring festival, but they ate only half and left the other half over. Da Meng, do you know why?

Da Meng: Because they want to have abundance year after year!

Wen Xiaoxi: What does this mean, exactly?

Da Meng: This year's fish you'll eat, but won't finish it, you'll eat the rest next year. The Chinese pronunciation of the saying "niannian you yu" means both having fish and a surplus every year. People hope that their lives will be getting better and better, so much so that they have food leftovers. Therefore, they say "niannian you yu" during every spring festival.

Jiang Yihua: Isn't that interesting! Anything else?

Da Meng: There's a lot. For example, the Chinese eat "tangyuan" during the Spring Festival. "Yuan" not only means "round" as in round glutinous rice balls, it also means "reunite with family members", so by eating "tangyuan", they hope that they can have a family reunion. Tangyuan are sweet, so eating them also implies the hope that all family members may lead a happy life, as sweet as "tangyuan". Another instance is the black sesame rice cake that is eaten during the Mid-Autumn Festival. These cakes are as big and as round as the moon during this festival; round again refers to expressing the wish of a family reunion. The cakes are made from glutinous rice; they are sweet and sticky. They are eaten in the hope that after consumption, all family members may stick together and do not part.

Jiang Yihua: Don't you eat moon cakes during the Mid-autumn Festival?

Da Meng: You're right. People from the North eat moon cakes, the Sichuanese traditionally eat black sesame rice cakes, but now a lot of them also eat moon cakes.

Wen Xiaoxi: Why do the Chinese like family reunions so much?

Da Meng: Because there used to be many wars and the people thought that if the family can come together safe and sound, then that is the greatest happiness of life. Today, there aren't any wars, but "family reunion" has become one of China's traditional family values.

Part 2 【 Food Associated with the 24 Solar Terms 】

Wen Xiaoxi: I want to eat moon cakes; let's go buy some.

Da Meng: Now it isn't the time for moon cakes; you won't find them.

Wen Xiaoxi: What do you mean?

Da Meng: Confucius said, "Don't eat when the time's not come". This means that you can't eat the foods that are not of this season.

Wen Xiaoxi: Why not?

Da Meng: Because the food in different seasons isn't the same. For example, tomatoes are summer food. Tomatoes in July have twice as much vitamin C as tomatoes in January. Spinach is winter food. The spinach in winter is eight times as nutritious than summer spinach.

Wen Xiaoxi: I got it. In the future, I won't eat when the time's not come.

Da Meng: Other than different foods during different seasons, traditional Chinese medicine believes that the human body and the seasons are closely connected with each other. The weather changes with the seasons and so do our bodies' needs, so we should eat different foods.

The Chinese divide the year into 24 solar terms according to changes in the weather. The Beginning of Spring is the first of the 24 solar terms, where winter will soon be over, and spring will soon arrive. Day time is getting longer and longer, the sun is warmer and warmer, and vegetables begin to grow buds. On that day, the Chinese make spring rolls out of these buds to celebrate the arrival of spring. They gift these spring rolls to their friends and hope that everyone may get even more food next year. On Rain Water, the Sichuanese eat potted preserved pork; on Pure Brightness, affine cudweed, by making boiled weed balls out of them; on Winter Solstice, lamb, so they will not feel the cold during the entirety of winter; Lesser Cold is the coldest day of the year. On this day, you are advised to eat eight-treasured rice porridge, so you can better keep yourself warm.

词语

幸 福	Xìngfú happiness	庆 祝	qìngzhù celebrate

bù 部	(measure word for films etc.)
nián nián yǒu yú 年 年 有 余	May you have abundance year after year! (an auspicious saying for the Lunar New Year, said during the Spring Festival)
tuán tuán yuán yuán 团 团 圆 圆	round and round; all round
nián 黏	sticky; glutinous
píng píng ān ān 平 平 安 安	safe and sound

shèng 剩	be left (over); remain
shèng yú 剩 余	surplus; remainder
zhàn zhēng 战 争	war
chuán tǒng 传 统	traditional
guān niàn 观 念	thought; concept; ideology

bèi 倍	times; -fold
wéi shēng sù 维 生 素	vitamin
àn zhào 按 照	according to; on the basis of
bā bā 粑 粑	wafer; -ball

yíng yǎng 营 养	nutrition
nèn 嫩	tender; delicate
bǎo nuǎn 保 暖	keep warm; protect against the cold

专有名词

1. 春节 / Chūn Jié / Spring Festival; Chinese New Year

2. 中秋节 / Zhōng Qiū Jié / Mid-Autumn Festival

3. 孔子 / Kǒngzǐ / Confucius

4. 雨水 / Yǔ Shuǐ / Rain Water

5. 清明 / Qīng Míng / Pure Brightness

6. 冬至 / Dōng Zhì / Winter Solstice

7. 小寒　/ Xiǎo Hán / Lesser Cold

8. 八宝粥　/ Bā Bǎo Zhōu /babaozhou; rice congee made with red beans, lotus seeds, longan, red dates, nuts, etc.

思　考

1. 除了文中提到的节日，还是哪些节日有特别的食物？为什么要吃这些食物？

2. 请举例说明在你们国家有哪些节日，有什么特别的食物。主要介绍一两种。

3. 你听过中国的二十四节气吗？它是根据什么来划分的？食物跟二十四节气有什么关系？

4. 除了文中提到的几个节气，还有什么节气有特别的食物？请举例说明。

立春
2月3-5日

雨水
2月18-20日

惊蛰
3月5-7日

立夏
5月5-7日

小满
5月20-22日

芒种
6月5-7日

立秋
8月7-9日

处暑
8月22-24日

白露
9月7-9日

立冬
11月7-8日

小雪
11月22-23日

大雪
12月6-8日

春分
3 月 20-22 日

清明
4 月 4-6 日

谷雨
4 月 19-21 日

夏至
6 月 21-22 日

小暑
7 月 6-8 日

大暑
7 月 22-24 日

秋分
9 月 22-24 日

寒露
10 月 8-9 日

霜降
10 月 23-24 日

冬至
12 月 21-23 日

小寒
1 月 5-7 日

大寒
1 月 20-21 日

参考文献
[References]

[1] 车辐 . 川菜杂谈 [M]. 成都：四川出版集团，四川文艺出版社，2011.

[2] 姚伟均 . 长江流域的地理环境与饮食文化 [J]. 中国文化研究，2002(1).

[3] 华国梁 . 中国饮食文化 [M]. 大连：东北财经大学出版社，2002.

〔附 录〕
〔Appendix〕

关于味道		麻、辣、咸、鲜、香、酸、甜
关于 火锅	锅底	红汤锅、清汤锅、鸳鸯锅
	菜	毛肚、鸭肠、肥牛、嫩牛肉、黄喉、老肉片、郡花、鱼、肉丸、香菇、西红柿、菠菜
	蘸料	油碟、干碟
关于调料		辣椒、辣椒面、辣椒油、花椒、花椒面、豆瓣酱、醋、糖、盐、胡椒
		芝麻油、蒜泥、葱花、香菜、蒜苗、大葱、蚝油、豆豉、酱
		酸菜、泡椒
关于味道		麻辣、酸辣、甜辣、鱼香、怪味
关于做法		炒、煮、烧、烫、炖

①面：四川话，意思是粉末状的东西。辣椒面就是用干红辣椒磨成的粉末。花椒面就是用干花椒磨成的粉末。

面：Sichuan dialect, meaning powdery things. Dried chili pepper powder refers to red chili peppers grounded into powder; the same principle applies to dried Sichuan pepper powder.

Flavors		ma, spicy, salty, umami, fragrant, sour, sweet
Hot Pot	soup base	red soup pot, clear soup pot, mandarin duck pot[1]
	ingredients	tripe, duck intestine, beef slices, tender beef, aorta, marbled meat slices, duck gizzard, fish, meatballs, mushrooms, tomatoes, spinach
	dips	oily, dry
Seasoning		chili pepper, dried chili pepper powder, chili oil, Sichuan pepper, dried Sichuan pepper powder, chili bean paste, vinegar, sugar, salt, black pepper
		sesame oil, mashed garlic, chopped green onion, coriander, garlic bolt, green Chinese onion, oyster sauce, fermented black soybeans, soy sauces
		pickled cabbage, pickled pepper
Flavor types		hot and tingling, hot and sour, hot and sweet, yuxiang, guaiwei
Preparation methods		stir-frying, boiling, braising, blanching, stewing

① Hot pot with a divider, containing spicy broth on one side and mild broth on the other. "Yuan" and "yang" respectively stand for male and female mandarin ducks. In traditional Chinese culture, mandarin ducks are believed to be lifelong couples, unlike other species of ducks. Hence they are regarded as a symbol of conjugal affection and fidelity.

图书在版编目（CIP）数据

成都印象／西南财经大学 汉语国际推广成都基地著 —成都：西南财经
大学出版社，2019.7
（走进天府系列教材）
ISBN 987-7-5504-3776-0

Ⅰ.①成… Ⅱ.①西… Ⅲ.①汉语—对外汉语教学—教材②成都—
概况 Ⅳ.①H 195.4②K 927.11
中国版本图书馆 CIP 数据核字（2018）第 241717 号

走进天府系列教材：成都印象·吃川菜

ZOUJIN TIANFU XILIE JIAOCAI:CHENGDU YINXIANG · CHI CHUANCAI

西南财经大学 汉语国际推广成都基地 著

策　　划：王正好　何春梅
责任编辑：李　才
装帧设计：张艳洁
插　　画：辣点设计
责任印制：朱曼丽

出版发行	西南财经大学出版社（四川省成都市光华村街 55 号）
网　　址	http://www.bookcj.com
电子邮件	bookcj@ foxmail.com
邮政编码	610074
电　　话	028-87353785
照　　排	上海辣点广告设计咨询有限公司
印　　刷	四川新财印务有限公司
成品尺寸	170mm×240mm
印　　张	46.5
字　　数	875 千字
版　　次	2019 年 7 月第 1 版
印　　次	2019 年 7 月第 1 次印刷
印　　数	1—2050 套
书　　号	ISBN 978-7-5504-3776-0
定　　价	198.00 元（套）